Simone Drenkelfort
Rainer Tillmann
Ton Driessen
& Dick de Ruiter

Reiki&Sound

Binkey Kok Publications – Havelte/Holland

2nd. printing 2006

Text Simone Drenkelfort, Rainer Tillmann, Ton Driessen & Dick de Ruiter
Editing Valerie Cooper
Music Rainer Tillmann
Pictures & paintings Rainer Tillmann
Layout Jaap Koning

First published in 2005 by Binkey Kok Publications – Havelte/Holland
www.binkeykok.com
E-mail info@binkeykok.com

ISBN90-74597-95-5

CONTENTS

I – INTRODUCTION

Reiki is a comprehensive healing method that excels by virtue of its simplicity, by itself as well as in addition to other similar therapies. It works for everyone who is willing to develop him- or herself and who takes inner growth seriously.

Because Reiki is currently practiced mostly by women, it is our hope to raise some interest in men as well with this book and CD. We would like to encourage more men to develop their feminine side, for the well-being of all.

Reiki is a way of dealing with universal energy, or in Japanese, *ki*. In this method, the energy is transmitted through the positioning of the Reiki giver's hands. The Reiki giver does not cure the recipient of this energy, but is only functioning as a portal. It is the receiver of this energy who—consciously or not—does the trick; his or her body and mind receives the nourishment of the transmitted *ki* in order to regain balance. In this process, the dis-eases that typically originate from disharmony in the body and mind will diminish or even disappear. Because of the fact that the physical body is replenished, the emotional body feels better as well. It also works the other way around: when your emotional body is feeling fine, your physical body will also feel better. And this creates an upward spiral toward healing. A positive change will occur within your own self, as well as in everything you do. And this in return has its effect on all the people around you.

Every human has the power to utilize this energy, to literally pass it on. Just think about where your hands are drawn to when a child you care for has tripped and fallen: right to the painful area. There's no need for full knowledge of this healing method; it is an in-born talent, and every living being has it. What you are doing unconsciously for the child in the caring caress, you do consciously in giving Reiki.

This book provides a concise introduction to a very wide-ranging and deep subject, which has been described in numerous books; so we lay no claims to its completeness.

We will introduce you to this wonderful system that springs from a well of timeless, gentle, and compassionate wisdom. You will learn about its links to other healing modalities, its background, about the various initiations the therapist goes through, and finally we will explain the Reiki healing connection with the singing bowls music on the enclosed CD, which has been created especially as a harmonizing background for a Reiki session.

And it may well be that this book will take you on your first step toward experiencing Reiki for your health, your mental stability, and eventually your spiritual growth as well.

In addition to offering here a first look at Reiki for beginners, with a description of the Reiki healer's motivations and methods, this book also provides a versatile tool for initiated Reiki givers. Besides holding a treasure of basic information that

Reiki practitioners can offer their clients to read, the special sounds of the CD will tremendously enrich their treatments.

– Simone Drenkelfort / Rainer Tillmann
Spring 2005

霊

気

Reiki

2 – WHAT IS REIKI?

Look, and it can't be seen.
Listen, and it can't be heard.
Reach, and it can't be grasped.

Above, it isn't bright.
Below, it isn't dark.
Seamless, unnamable, it returns to the realm of nothing.
Form that includes all forms, image without an image, subtle, beyond
all conception.

Approach it and there is no beginning;
follow it and there is no end.

– *Tao Te Ching*, Chapter 14

Some thousands of years ago in Tibet, there was a group of seers who kept a still older secret: a secret that probably was a relic from the lost continent of Atlantis. After the disappearance of this vast continent, in various areas on our Earth there were still groups of people who preserved the heritage of the lost empire. These were the architects and masterminds behind the mystical structures such as the

Great Pyramid of Gizeh and the mysterious temples in South America and Asia.

One of these secrets contained a technique originating from the fact that every human being is able to channel the universal life energy known in the Far East as *ki*, and let it flow through to the body as a healing source. Anyone can be a channel for this inexhaustible energy, *Rei-ki*, in order to pass it on to others *with love*. And that is the very essence of this therapy.

What exactly *ki* is, no one can explain, for it entails describing something that is indescribable. The *Tao Te Ching* offers an impression of how imageless it actually is, beyond any interpretation. Any sketched image, any vision, or insight from anyone is just as valuable as someone else's. Attempts to explain Reiki in a scientific way cannot be absolute, although the book *The Field* by Lynne McTaggart offers a promising description.

Although remains of the ancient knowledge can still be found in other Eastern therapies such as yoga and Ayurveda in India and acupuncture in China, most of it unfortunately got lost over the course of time.

It was a Japanese school teacher, Dr. Mikao Usui (Kyoto, 1865), who during the second half of the 19th century rediscovered the basic system and named it Reiki. But this was no maverick development on his part. For more than twenty years, he studied all kinds of healing methods and *sutras* (Buddhist teachings), which brought to his awareness a number of age-old symbols and syllables that appeared to have a directly demonstrable effect on the body, particularly on the nervous

system. He transformed his experiences into a system that since has been refined and supplemented for many years.

After a period of profound meditation, it became clear to Dr. Usui that he had a mission to propagate this system in order to utilize this inexhaustible life energy for the healing of people and animals. Until he left our realm in 1926, he taught these basics of Reiki therapy. Other masters followed in his footsteps: Hayashi, Takata, and Furumoto. Yet Reiki was introduced to the West as late as the 1970s, and ever since has been going through a tremendous growth. Unfortunately, as with every new trend, it experienced indiscriminate proliferation as well, and the

Dr. Mikao Usui

ensuing pitfalls thereof, with people who would ask for huge amounts of money for the simple initiations.

What *is* observable though, even scientifically, are the effects of working with *ki*. Many students and masters who spent time and energy on treating themselves and others, are reaching the same conclusion. Passing on Reiki relaxes body and mind and supports the self-healing ability of the receiver. Reiki does not heal— even the Reiki giver cannot be considered a healer. The receiver of Reiki determines consciously or unconsciously how to handle this energy. In other words, when someone is open to the flow of *ki* through his or her whole being (the physical and emotional bodies), this may result in healing or acceptance. Some improvement will always occur and this often leads to a greater awareness and change of views, lifestyle, and habits.

Reiki may be used as a stand-alone healing method, but you can also support other therapies with it. When you get prescribed medicine from your doctor, Reiki will improve its effectiveness, so you may be able to use the medication for a shorter period of time. Of course, never do this on your own; always seek the guidance of your physician. When you get help from a mental health institution or counselor, a psychiatrist, or psychologist, you will soon reach a better state. When your arm is broken and you treat it with Reiki (right through the plaster cast) you will notice the fracture heals better. And there are many more examples in which Reiki works as a very supportive method.

Another very important note regarding this: all healing methods are for the benefit of all sentient beings (people, animals, and plants); there is no one therapy that is the only right one. As soon as someone distinguishes a therapy as the only right one and at the same time judges others as faulty, it is not advisable to follow through with this person's therapeutic ministrations.

Although Reiki goes back to ancient principles, it is not something that should be shrouded in mystery. Anyone can learn to do it, provided his or her goals are always morally pure, without ego gratification, or pursuit of personal gain. This is often emphasized during the various stages of initiation.

Reiki, the universal life energy, is available to everyone, because it surrounds us always and everywhere. And it is good to stop and think about the fact that we are already using this energy mostly in an unconscious way. When we have a headache, we automatically lay our hands on our head or on our temples. When our stomach aches, our hands are drawn to the belly. We do this intuitively, without thinking. In Reiki, the healing energy is also applied through the hands.

Intuition, a typically feminine faculty that can be nourished in men as well, plays an important part in Reiki. Another equally important starting point in Reiki is the subconscious regulation of the quantity of energy a person can handle, which results in an energy level that can never be too much.

Because of the book *The Da Vinci Code*, literally millions of people today are for the first time becoming aware of the undeniable transition from the Age of Pisces to the more androgynous Aquarius era, which is now in progress. Reiki is another example of a healing method that is a hallmark of this age: the use of *soft, loving heart energy* that will cause so many positive changes in the coming decennia: on a physical level, the mental level, the social level, and even on a political level.

Like love itself, the term "Reiki" may never be explained or tangible. But everyone who has gotten in touch with it understands very well what it is all about. And when the effects turn out to be favorable to everyone and therefore to the whole world, then it surely must be in the Tao: a balanced way.

3 – THE REIKI DEGREES

The Reiki system that originated from the Usui method consists of three consecutive "degrees." Every degree in this arrangement is completely autonomous; you don't need to take all three degrees in order to become a Reiki healer.

An initiation is not a definite requirement, but it does provide the Reiki giver very precise tools to access the universal life energy. Those tools also protect him or her from negative external influences, and prevent the practitioner from using his or her own energy, which would result in emptiness and fatigue. Someone who gives Reiki with a pure attitude will also be energized and will feel fine and strong after a session.

Initiations in Reiki are an important part of a Reiki course. The initiation is a fine way of symbolizing the cleansing of the channels, so the life energy may flow freely through your body once again. Sometimes the initiation is surrounded with a lot of mystery. We would rather consider it as a mystical, curious, very powerful undertaking, like the Christening, taking marriage vows, or rituals that mark other important turning points in your life. The more aware your are in this step, the more powerfully the energy will flow within you. Proper introduction and coaching in this by the initiating Reiki master is indispensable.

Most of us automatically use willpower in order to get better when we are ill. And sometimes the willpower is there, but there is also a lack of energy. By replenishing this (for example, by giving treatments), the sick person will be able to fight once more.

A person who gives treatments is only human and will not always be able to perform a miracle, even though miracles are not completely impossible. We cannot expect that illness can always be prevented or healed.

Furthermore, it is important to know that because of the gradual and soft radiance that is provided in a Reiki treatment, a gradual and calm healing will be the result. So there is no rush, or dramatic result, which is actually antithetical to the gentle rebalancing that Reiki can achieve.

You could compare the initiation process with the fine tuning of a radio, or the precise positioning of a satellite dish.

The ways of treatment and the Reiki courses according to the Usui System improve and promote mutual contact among people. It literally and figuratively brings them together. It is beautiful to see how the one who is treated relaxes and changes.

During the initiation, the person learns how to be continuously connected with the Reiki force in order to heal him- or herself and others. Basic techniques are passed on, including the spiritual regimen of the Reiki work.

Dr. Usui believed that he ought to offer his patients a certain attitude adjustment toward life, in order to prolong the healing process. He laid down this attitude toward life in five rules, or life wisdom. They are an important part of the practical Reiki application.

These rules, positively formulated and completed in the course of time, are as follows:

* Feel free and happy today.

* Enjoy yourself today.

* Today you will be taken care of.

* Live consciously in the now.

* Accept your blessings with gratitude.

* Honor your parents, teachers, and the elderly.

* Earn an honest living.

* Be thankful for everything and radiate love to all living things.

These rules do not have a moral subtext; they are primarily meant to remind you to constantly hold your way of life to the light. A way of consciously dealing with this wisdom cannot be eliminated from the process of Reiki; it is part and parcel of it, just like the initiations themselves.

Touching is healthy, very healthy. Touching is essential to our well-being. But how do we introduce it into this afraid-of-touch society?

Through Reiki, this is very easily accomplished and satisfying. Reiki is an unconditional way of touching. During a treatment you will feel loved, accepted, important, and cared for. These feelings are nourishing to your being. They are a way to allow yourself the chance to open up, meaning you are giving yourself a chance to let the very best of you to sprout. Do not expect anything from another, but be happy with anything you receive.

All these degrees and initiations increase and amplify the current of universal energy. In every session, this energy will flow through the hands of the Reiki practitioner into the body of the receiving person, toward the areas that need it the most. It equally affects the physical, the mental, and the soul level, because Reiki is a force born out of love, not a capturing force. Reiki flows by way of the heart!

The First Degree

In the first Reiki degree, the initiate is "attuned" with the energy by an experienced Reiki master—someone who has passed the third degree—so his or her channel is opened. Every person is a channel; it is simply a matter of "turning on" the switch. The student then learns how to do a complete body treatment, on him- or herself and others.

The Second Degree

During this initiation, the student receives the three spiritual symbols and/or sounds through which the energy can be further invigorated. Through thought power, which also allows distance healing, the Reiki practitioner is able to heal beyond time and space. This may seem unbelievable to our Western minds, but try to think about the way image and sound are sent by a transmitting station, invisibly through space via satellite, and finally are picked up by a satellite dish, to be transformed into the same image and sound again. Isn't this just as unbelievable? You really can compare Reiki transmission with this, however, the Reiki power, although in use for ages, works by way of mechanisms which have yet to be tested and investigated by science.

Through this attunement, the Reiki flow of energy gains considerable strength, and can be directed more accurately to specific goals or body parts.

The Third Degree

This grade contains initiation into the so-called Master degree. Here, the Master symbol is given to the initiate. This degree is also important for your own personal growth. A door will be opened to the world of meditation. After this attunement, you can also initiate others into the first degree.

Within this degree is the initiation to mastery: here all knowledge about the passing on of knowledge and energy activation is given to the initiate.

The beauty of Reiki is that the energy flows *through* the Reiki practitioner; there is none of the energy drain that often happens with other methods. The practitioner is just channeling the life energy. Reiki flows through the crown of the head toward the heart center of the practitioner, and from there to his or her hands into the receiver. In the process, the practitioner will always take in a little life energy, too. Repeated Reiki sessions will secure a growth toward more love, truth, trust, insight, and freedom from fear.

This automatically implies a growing insight into the various ways Reiki can be offered to a client, depending on the practitioner's measure of personal growth.

Many people initially go the Reiki way to resolve physical an emotional discomforts. After treatment or training, chances are likely that there will be a spontaneous change, which often will be more readily noticed by others than by the Reiki recipient him- or herself. The relaxation that almost always occurs is the first thing that is evident. Because of this relaxed state it is possible to quietly look at your own situation and relationships—in short, all of your life circumstances and considerations. The already-mentioned Usui principles, which are taught during a Reiki course, will also contribute to this. You may realize you are able to do more than you thought possible—not only in your daily activities, but also in developing and appreciating abilities and capacities that you may have previously attributed to "more talented people." Everything that is popularly designated as "paranormal" or "psychic" turns out to be within everyone's reach. So it is much more "normal" than we thought it to be. Dealing with Reiki, by treating yourself and others the Reiki way, will enhance your intuitive abilities.

Here also lies a responsibility for the Reiki master: to be able to support others in the understanding of their own ability, their own inner strength. Then it becomes obviously clear that we take responsibility for our own lives. When you act from this center, you also will feel the "Force." Then you will not have to say: "Yes, but the other…" No need to, because you are free, no longer dependant on what another person does or does not! You are free to make your own choices. You are free to feel happy. You look at what you are able to do, who you are, and what you do. The results of your actions are also at your own expense; you do not have to burden someone else with this. You are no longer part of the problem, but part of the solution.

Someone else will not make you happy, you will. But someone else may take part of your happiness.

It is good to realize that we may enjoy life, that it does not have to be a wrestling contest.[1] It is good to realize our common origin, the mutual connection between us through this. It is good to know we can be of help to each other.

Often Reiki is considered to be an energy that is available only when you have passed the initiation ritual of the Usui system of Reiki healing. We consider this a bit more differentiating, after our experience with Reiki initiations and treatments. From the very moment of conception, everyone and everything is impregnated with life's energy: How else would we stay alive? When we are feeling well, when we are relaxed, there is no reason why the *ki* force should not flow freely through our bodies. Perhaps that is why they say: "the more I relax, the more I accomplish!"

Often we are physically and emotionally unable to cope with the unhealthy tension we meet in daily life. In the never-ending pursuing of greater material wealth and prosperity, assuming that is where real happiness comes from, we run into ourselves, sooner or later. Chances are that we get overworked, resulting in numerous ailments and defects. Our energy is interrupted. Many of the resulting problems are being dealt with by the traditional medical science by trying to prevent or solve them, but often this remains no more than a fight against symptoms. By clearing the self-made blocks of tension, fears, and walls between us and the other, the *ki* will be able to flow freely once more. Not only within us, but also around us. The more we liberate ourselves of whatever literally holds us down, the more we will feel better and the more this will radiate around us. So, taking good care of yourself means also taking care of what (or who) surrounds you.

In this we have a choice. You may reinforce those choices by consciously experiencing a Reiki session and/or initiation(s).

4 – THE REIKI ENVIRONMENT

The right conditions during a Reiki session will positively reinforce the overall experience. Of course, Reiki will flow even without these special and supporting arrangements, but practitioners and recipients report that using things to create a relaxing atmosphere in order to support the healing process makes a significant difference in the quality of the experience.

Warm light, a comfortable room temperature, easy, loose clothing, and a correct reclining position are self-evident necessities during a Reiki session. Additionally, you may use essential oils or incense to energetically cleanse the room, and of course the use of appropriate music may be the most important component of a Reiki session. For this reason the music on the CD with this book has been created.

Before (and after) the session, the practitioner needs to wash his or her hands, and then rub them warm or hold them near a candle flame. We must emphasize that these actions need to be seen as purely ritual. In a similar mindset, the Reiki practitioner will cleanse him- or herself of other people's energy, wash off psychic tension, and absorb fresh, clean life energy. Rituals provide hope and trust in the healing process—they appeal to the subconscious mind. Moreover, there might be a kind of "energy pollution" surrounding the practitioner and the client; by rinsing the hands, this can be avoided.[2] A purely physical reason for washing one's hands is that hot, clammy hands cannot transfer the Reiki energy flow as well.

Before the beginning of a session, all jewelry needs to be removed, especially those with precious stones and metals. Even earrings are not allowed. Watches and all electronic equipment like mobile phones need to be kept out of the room.

Have the person who wants a session lie down on a table that is high enough so you may sit at ease next to it and can move freely around it. Lay your hands carefully and in a relaxed way on the person's body. If needed, use a cushion to support your arms. Move your hands one by one, in order to keep contact with the person's body. After the session, you let the person "wake up" slowly, for instance by gently massaging his or her back. Then the person can sit for a moment, while you offer him or her an extra glass of water. This is to drain the waste the body will release as a result of the treatment.

We use a number of hand positions on the head, the front, and the back. Altogether there are about fourteen positions, depending on the size of your own hands and the size of the body you are working on. The significant aspect of our particular method of teaching Reiki is to enable you to avoid *thinking* about how you ought to do it. Above all, the most important thing is the touch itself, not whether your fingers are adjusted like this or that. The *form* is less important than the *intention*. This intention means being there for the person and the handing on of Reiki.

Many books about Reiki often are packed with ways of treatment, together with loads of how-to pictures or drawings. This may lead to misapprehension. You simply cannot do it wrong.

We limit ourselves here to an example of a basic session, so you will get the idea of what we do.

As an introduction to the treatment, an affirmation or a short prayer is usually spoken. Sometimes a certain kind of calming breathing technique will be sufficient. This enables the Reiki practitioner to focus and create the desired relaxed atmosphere.

Then the session starts with the practitioner laying his or her hands on or above various areas of the recipient's body. Often a *chakra balancing* (see chapter 5) to even out the aura will be the first part of the treatment. *Whole-body Reiki* (total treatment) includes movements of the hands, usually from the top of the head toward the legs, and then in a circular movement near the head (always without touching the body). At the end of the session, one hand will be moved pretty quickly from the lower back toward the head.

Next, the session is completed with certain actions that make sure the "energy valve" is disconnected the right way, after which the practitioner consciously takes in some extra energy once more.

A complete session may last for one hour—the total playing time of the CD is synchronized to this duration.

5 – REIKI AND CHAKRA BALANCING

The word *chakra* comes from the Sanskrit, meaning "wheel" or "whirling." The seven main chakras are energy vortexes along the spine (of our energy body) and in the head. In addition to these, there are other chakras, in the hands, feet, and in the spleen area.[3]

The chakras are part of our personal "energy network" which is part of our *aura*. The energy body can be seen as a kind of blueprint, holding all the information for the right functioning of our physical body. Reiki works within the framework of this energy body, causing a stronger flow of the universal energy directly to our organs and tissues.

Our vitality and development of self-assuredness, as well as our spiritual awareness, depend on how active and open the chakras are: the more energy is able to flow through the chakras, the more healthy we are.

When we perform the basic postures and movements of Reiki, we nourish the seven main chakras as well, activating them at the same time. We can support this even further by imagining how a chakra is opening and radiating. Visualizing the corresponding colors can help, too.

During self-treatment as well as during the treatment of others, it is recommended in most cases to balance the chakras first and then to even out the aura. For this purpose, we lay our hands on two different chakras and keep them there until the energy sensation in both hands is felt equally. The heart chakra serves as a mediator with regard to all other chakras, which can be paired as follows: 1st and 7th chakra; 2nd and 6th chakra; 3rd and 5th chakra.

The timbre of the CD has the root chakra tone (tone C sharp) as a basic tone, in order to keep the practitioner energetically grounded during the whole session.

Below you will see the colors belonging to the seven chakras. The colors can be visualized in the area of the chakras inside the body during the Reiki balancing.

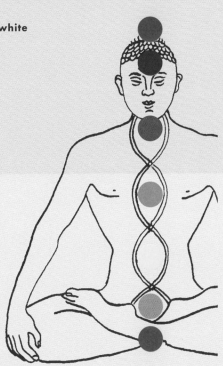

7 Crown chakra – Light violet/white

6 Brow chakra – Indigo/violet

5 Throat chakra – Clear blue

4 Heart chakra – Pink/green

3 Solar plexus chakra – Yellow

2 Sacral chakra – Orange

1 Root chakra – Red

6 – BASIC POSITIONS

The first degree Reiki initiation also involves the transmission of the knowledge of applying the twelve basic positions or hand attitudes, along with six secondary positions.

The exact description and effects on body, mind, and soul are beyond the limits of this little book, so here we would like to refer to the books in reading list at the back of the book.

When all the basic positions are subsequently done, we call it a *full-body treatment*, and it takes about one hour. As an example, we have provided illustrations of hand positions for the head, with six additional positions for self treatment.

Example hand position for the head

This is one of our favorite positions. It connects and balances the right and left hemispheres of the brain. We know from experience that those who suffer from headaches love this position. With both hands parallel beneath the back of the head, often the ballast (fears and sorrows) will be eliminated. It can also provide relief from headaches, asthma, and circulatory problems.

Another hands-on position for the head is when the hands are covering both halves of the face. This position can be used for a cold, sinus problems, eye complaints, allergies, tiredness, and a general feeling of malaise.

Yet another position is with the hands on both sides over the ears, with the fingertips touching the jaw and neck. Here the healing energy is directed toward the throat area and can help with equilibrium problems such as vertigo and hearing problems like tinnitus.

For the body there are many possible hand positions on the chest and belly, as well as on the back. Examples of areas where Reiki may be of help are: to strengthen the immune system, the lymph glands, the heart, the lungs, kidneys, gonads, and digestion; elimination of toxins; and alleviation of allergies.

Naturally, it is of the utmost importance to point out the fact that the system has it limitations. When someone has serious complaints that need immediate med-

ical care, direct and efficient professional help must of course be sought. Like so many other therapies that work with body energy, Reiki must be seen as a catalyst enabling the body to bring about sufficient self-healing power, not as a replacement for necessary allopathic medical care. Common sense in this matter is advised.

In this context, we want to emphasize that Reiki will reduce the negative side-effects of medicines, and that with continuous Reiki treatments, the healing process after a medical operation can be improved and accelerated. Scientific research has demonstrated that Reiki has the power to increase the percentage of hemoglobin and hematocrit in the blood. The beneficial effects on the thymus gland plays an especially important role in this matter. This hormone gland produces numerous antibodies (t-lymphocytes) that work throughout the whole body via the bloodstream, but it also has a direct connection with the production of certain brain products, like endorphins, which make us feel better. This is one of the reasons why people at the end of a Reiki session often feel so fine, relaxed, and cheerful.

And now those results can be further reinforced with the sounds of the singing bowls on the CD, because these have similar effects!

7 – SELF-TREATMENT

Every Reiki practitioner will begin with the self-treatment, because this influences his or her daily life in a very direct and impressive way. Because of this, over time, as practitioners, we learn to find peace and rejuvenation within ourselves; we become more relaxed and better able to resist being pushed out of balance by the outside world.

Because of this very reason, you should practice self-treatment Reiki on a regular basis. A good suggestion is to do a short self-treatment in the morning in bed, directly after waking up. Because the chances are high that you will fall asleep again while doing this, just do the hands-on treatment as briefly as possible, yet as long as needed. You may choose to lay your hands only on specific areas, or do your entire front side, as shown in the pictures. You may choose any or all the positions you can handle while lying down. Experience shows that the chakra treatment is the most effective one here.

Reiki can be received while lying down, sitting, or standing. Self-treatment results in vitalizing your whole energy system, and mobilizing your self-healing powers. Your body is detoxified and because of this cleansing process, the way toward mental and physical development is cleared. You may become more intuitive and even develop clairvoyant abilities. Under the guidance of an experienced Reiki practitioner, all of this can be guided into the right direction. So it is important to investigate the background and motivations of the practitioner who does your initiation(s).

The hand positions for self-treatment are of course different and more limited compared to the treatment of another person. Below you will see some examples of hand positions during a self-treatment.

Self-treatment for the eyes, sinuses, and brain nerves; relaxes the entire head.

Self-treatment on the acupuncture points here on the head, connected to: heart, stomach, kidneys, liver, gallbladder, and intestines.

Self-treatment for psychic complaints such as fear, shock, hyperventilation, difficulty swallowing. Results in a clear head.

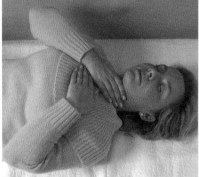

This position can also be done while lying down.

Self-treatment for the heart and solar plexus chakras. Affects heart, lungs, blood, circulation, skin, spleen, gall-bladder, digestion, and the autonomic nervous system.

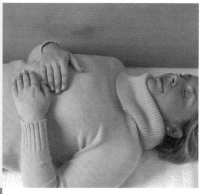

Self-treatment for the sacral and root chakras. Affects the entire uro-genital area (bladder, kidneys, reproductive and sex organs) and intestines.

8 – REIKI AND HOLISTIC MEDICINE

Reiki can be easily and effectively combined with other therapies, such as sound massage. The person to be treated lies down with big loudspeakers on both sides or at the feet, and is "massaged" by special harmonic sounds, which results in relaxation, cleansing, and recharging. Directly afterwards, you may give Reiki to the person, placing your hands on previously determined areas of the person's body. This is often a very pleasant and intensive experience.

You may also proceed the other way around: I tested this sound massage with my clients, and first gave a whole-body Reiki treatment and followed that with a "sound bath," working with singing bowls placed directly on the body. And, naturally, the CD can also be used as a background sound healing *during* the whole Reiki session.

Furthermore, there are other therapies that can be combined with Reiki, such as Aura Soma, gem and crystal therapy, Bach flower remedies, homeopathy, and aromatherapy.

With the use of crystal therapy,[4] the practitioner lays the stones, often quartz crystals, on various places of the body, sometimes on acupuncture points. The crystals are considered to be concentrated forms of harmonizing energy that can be used, for example, to release blocks (rose quartz), improve body functions (clear quartz) or to clear one's mind and eliminate fears (amethyst).

Quartz crystal is also utilized during Reiki meditations, with the stones held in both hands. In the Reiki meditation position, with palms and soles against each other, there is a "closed circuit" of energy that can be mentally directed toward a desired area, or may be used to charge the whole energy system.

Bach flower and homeopathic remedies also function at a similar, vibrational energy level as Reiki. So, like many other holistic therapies, Reiki works as a method to increase the effectiveness of these remedies.

Aromatherapy is also often combined with Reiki. Aromatherapy involves using natural, high-quality essential oils that can sometimes be

used directly on the skin—such as sandalwood oil—or in water, such as in a bath-tub or a vaporizer, whereby the vapor spreads in the air and is inhaled. Lavender, sage, and patchouli can be effectively used in this manner.

In our times, when people are increasingly interested in natural healing methods, Reiki is a very fine and complete method. Your intuition will grow, you will become more open and alive, and help spread more happiness and optimism.

If you have become curious and would like to lose yourself in the whole mat-ter, just glance through our reading list at the back of this book, and intuitively find a book that appeals to you!

9 – REIKI AND MUSIC

No doubt, the use of music and sound is the most simple, and at the same time the most effective, way to create a comprehensive Reiki session. By experimenting and exchanging information with other Reiki practitioners, we have created a CD that is appropriate for a complete Reiki session as well as for use during relaxation and meditation. Instead of "music," we prefer to use the phrase *permanent sound atmosphere* that literally harmonizes with the flow of energy during the Reiki session. The sounds complement the treatment; they become one whole experience.

An affirmation with such a Reiki-sound session could well be: *We are one with the sound, one with the universal life energy that we allow to flow through us, just like the sounds.*

As an attunement and preparation, the CD begins with the sounds of the Chinese Gu Zheng (a kind of zither; see chapter 12) and clear tones of singing bowls, evoking a feeling of space, warmth, and security.

Next, there is one uninterrupted piece of about sixty minutes (the average duration of a Reiki-sound session) with only singing bowls that have a very calming character, like the waves of the sea, rolling onto the beach (see chapter 10).

As a closure and an accompaniment of "coming back" to physical embodiment, you will hear again the light bowls along with the Chinese Gu Zheng, returning your awareness to the here and now.

The deep, basic tone you will hear throughout the whole recording—which also has a very calming and grounding effect—is produced by two large singing bowls. Intentionally we did *not* include "tinklers" at intervals in order to indicate the changing of hand positions. We determined to exclude this after consulting other Reiki practitioners. In our opinion, one should work intuitively and "in the flow," so there are no fixed periods for any position. Every body has unique healing requirements in terms of the time and focus directed toward it.

On this CD, we intentionally applied the effects of tones and sounds. Our hearing is our most sensitive sense organ, essentially more sensitive than, for instance, our sight or our taste. While the eye can perceive only a frequency range of about one octave, the ear is able to distinguish a range of almost ten octaves. So that is why we would like to present these sounds as an aid to, and enrichment for, growth on all levels.

6 – MUSICAL MANTRAS

The longest track of the CD was composed using the discoveries of the Swiss scientist and researcher Hans Cousto. This piece consists of sound ranges in minor chords, with a relaxing character.

The use of mantras is an Asiatic form of hymn of praise or a kind of prayer: a combination of words or just one word, sung or spoken, which is repeated over and over, until in the end the performer becomes one with the sound, so to speak. An example of such a mantra is:

OM MANE PADME HUM
(Tibetan mantra)

Within the framework of the therapeutic instrumental music on the CD, the musical ranges of tones being used "stand in for" the mantra. Here, these ranges with intervals are repeated as well, with now and then a little variation, but basically these are the same structures sounding over and over again in a timeless whole—exactly the way we would hear it in the intonation of classical Indian mantras.

The tone with a very relaxing effect on the deepest level is the so-called "yeartone," belonging to our planet earth, often named the "suntone" as well. It is a C-sharp major at 136.10 Hertz (32 times the octave). The tone is a representation of the "OM", the primeval vibration, the eternally sounding tone, as the Indians say. And it is the basic tone in which instruments in India are tuned, because it is the "Sadja," the "father of all tones."

So this C-sharp is also the basis for our Reiki CD and is created by the sounding of two large singing bowls[5] and is audible during the whole length of the recording.

Over this basic tone, other intervals in the minor key are played, in the keys C-sharp – E – G-sharp – c-sharp – e – g-sharp – c-sharp.

The relaxing and calming effect of this music has its particular effect because of the omission of intervals with a tense character, like those found in the major chords.[6] In order to emphasize the subtlety of the sounds, the tones D-sharp and high B are now and then added.

The OM—symbol of the primeval vibration

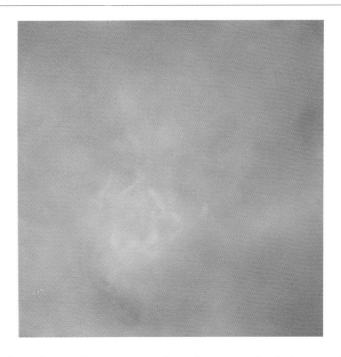

The color pink, as well as green, is traditionally associated with the heart chakra.
"Color-space-image" by Rainer Tillmann

Reiki works and flows mostly by way of the heart chakra. Likewise, this year- or suntone has for this CD and for Reiki a special meaning, because it has a connection with the level of the heart:

He who meditates on the suntone, he who becomes one with this tone,
will be filled with everything the sun represents in our consciousness:
light, clarity, joy, radiance, gratitude.

A Reiki treatment or self-treatment that is accompanied by music based on the suntone will give us an intense and complete experience of the universal life energy. It will also touch a special resonance within, of the song of sun and earth.

Singing bowls have been used in the Himalayas by shamans and monks, during rituals and offerings, as far back as living memory can record. The bowls also have played a role in sound support during meditations.

The bowls are struck with a felt hammer *or* rubbed along the rim with a stick, resulting in an uninterrupted basic tone with many harmonic overtones, just like those produced by rubbing the moistened rim of a crystal glass. These sounds are able to affect the chakras and to harmonize one's physical energy. Because of the calming effect that their pure, harmonic, overtone-rich sounds have on the awareness, singing bowls are able to balance

both brain hemispheres, resulting in an even deeper relaxation.

The sound of a struck singing bowl can last for minutes; this is made possible—according to the master handiwork of the metalsmith—by utilizing a special metal alloy, sometimes even of twelve different metals. It is a tone that will spread throughout the room, until suddenly one is not able to tell where it originally came from.

Sounds from another time and dimension

12 – THE GU ZHENG

The Gu Zheng is an ancient Chinese instrument with 21 strings. It is also called a Chinese zither and resembles, in shape and sound as well as the way it is played, the Japanese koto, but the koto has only 13 strings.

All 21 strings run over movable wooden bridges, which enables a very precise and pure tuning.

By pressing down on the strings just behind those bridges, the pitch can be slightly varied. With these modulations, the classic Chinese or Japanese melodious timbre is created.

The effects of this peculiar, ancient musical instrument are very relaxing, refined, and at the same time, clarifying and purifying. On the CD the Zheng is used at the start and as a closure of the Reiki session, in order to help gather one's thoughts, to direct one's concentration, and to induce a relaxed state of mind.

CD CONTENTS

1 – TUNING IN 4:04
2 – TREATMENT - SOUND MANTRAS 1:18:06
3 – COMING BACK 3:37

Total playing time: 75:30

The music is one continuous flow without interruption.

All music © 2005 by Rainer Tillmann

HOW TO LISTEN TO THE CD

In chapters 9 and 10 we already discussed the contents and structure of the Reiki CD.

This music is especially composed to be used as a background for a Reiki session, so the sounds should never be played too loud, but at a level so that the deep sounds of the basic tone, the suntone, can be clearly perceived. Should this not be the case, then try to emphasize these tones with the bass control knob on your equipment. In the reverse case, you can of course also reduce these tones if needed. This always depends on the quality and the size of the available sound equipment, especially the speakers. Also, take into account that every person reacts differently to lower frequencies. In most Reiki parlors there is only smaller playback equipment, therefore we produced a pretty powerful bass mix. So try to find out what best suits your room!

Naturally, you may also use this CD for other purposes, for instance as a background to meditation. But here, too, you need to adapt the sound volume to the purpose; it should always be pleasant to the ear, never too loud.

For the Reiki practitioner, a testing period at the outset may be necessary to determine in which way the sounds are best integrated into the whole practice. Some practitioners will use the CD before treatment and then give the Reiki in silence. Others will treat first and then play the CD afterwards as a relaxing period. But in most cases, the practitioner will choose to use it during the Reiki session.

After some experimentation, you will finally be able to successfully use the CD with any session.

We would love to hear about your own experience!

NOTES

1. Read Stuart Wilde, *Life Was Never Meant to Be a Struggle* (Denver, CO: White Dove International, 1987).
2. There are special liquids nowadays that can be used for this purpose, as a neutralizing spray. More information is available at *www.GlobalLight.net*.
3. You may read more about chakras in *Chakra Delight*, included in the Binkey Kok book/CD series. And for variety during the chakra treatment, you may work with the series of chakra tones on the CD with the 6th publication in this series, *Yoga & Sound* (vowels with overtone voice and singing bowls).
4. Another title in this book/CD series, *Crystal & Sound*, provides an overview of how to combine crystal therapy with singing bowls.
5. In another title in this series, *The Unique Singing Bowl.*, you will find out all about this technique and singing bowls.
6. These effects are explained in detail in the book & CD, *Yoga & Sound*.

READING LIST

Baginski, Bodo J. and Shalila Sharamon. *Reiki: Universal Life Energy.* Mendocino, CA: Life Rhythm, 1988.

Brennan, Barbara Ann. *Hands of Light: A Guide to Healing through the Human Energy Field.* New York: Bantam, 1988.

———. *Light Emerging: The Journey of Personal Healing.* New York: Bantam, 1993.

Cousto, Hans. *The Cosmic Octave.* Mendocino, CA: Life Rhythm, 2000.

———. *Klänge, Bilder, Welten.* Berlin: Simon & Leutner, 1989.

Huyser, Anneke. *Singing Bowl Exercises for Personal Harmony.* Havelte, Holland: Binkey Kok Publications, 2000.

Lübeck, Walter. *The Complete Reiki Handbook.* Twin Lakes, WI: Lotus Press, 1994.

———. *Rainbow Reiki.* Twin Lakes, WI: Lotus Press, 1997.

McTaggart, Lynne. *The Field: The Quest for the Secret Force of the Universe.* New York: HarperCollins, 2002.

Mitchell, Stephen, trans. *Tao Te Ching.* New York: Harper & Row, 1988.

Müller, Brigitte and Horst H. Gunther. *A Complete Book of Reiki Healing: Heal Yourself, Others, and the World Around You.* Mendocino, CA: Life Rhythm, 1995.

Stein, Diane. *Essential Reiki: A Complete Guide to an Ancient Healing Art.* Freedom, CA: Crossing Press, 1995.

Usui, Mikao. *The Original Reiki Handbook of Dr. Mikao Usui.* Twin Lakes, WI: Lotus Press, 1999.

Wilde, Stuart. *Life Was Never Meant to Be a Struggle.* Denver, CO: White Dove International, 1987.

RAINER TILLMANN

is a talented singing bowls player from Germany with many years of experience. He discovered the harmonizing effects of singing bowls in the 1980s, when he was still playing in a rock band. From then on he specialized as a meditation musician and performer. He created a series of touchingly beautiful singing bowls concerts on CD. He currently owns a collection of over 150 antique metal  and modern crystal bowls. Today he is one of the most versatile players, who effortlessly combines his art with healing. Apart from his skills as a musician, Rainer works as a painter as well. His clear, meditative "color-space images" are portrayed in this book. He had numerous exhibitions of his work in Germany and abroad, partly in combination with performances with his singing bowls and gongs, creating a "Color-sound-timbre" theme.

SIMONE DRENKELFORT

has been working for about ten years in the field of holistic healing. Her work as a "sound masseuse" and Reiki practitioner/teacher offers a good counterpart between heaven and earth, which she finds essential in balancing her profession as an airline stewardess with her healing practice. Simone also has an education in holistic massage therapy and is a "La Stone Practitioner."

DICK DE RUITER

has been a yoga teacher since 1969, and has specialized since 1980 in the harmonic possibilities of sound. In the 1970s, he introduced new age music to the Netherlands with his mail order business Sono Music of Silence and has offered numerous workshops about the effects of sound and special music in daily life. He writes and translates books on yoga, sound, and related subjects. He is also the author of the Binkey Kok Book & CD series.

TON DRIESSEN

We are gratefull to Ton Driessen, a Dutch Reiki master, who made an important contribution to the text of this book.

Other titles in this book/CD series from Binkey Kok:

THE UNIQUE SINGING BOWL
a divine exception in a world of music
ISBN 90-74597-46-7

CHAKRA DELIGHT
singing bowls for balancing the energy centers
ISBN 90-74597-49-1

THE HEALING TONES OF DIDGERIDOO
an invitation to a profound spiritual journey
ISBN 90-74597-48-3

HARMONIC OVERTONES
magical vibrations in voice and music
ISBN 90-74597-58-0

CRISTAL & SOUND
crystal singing bowls with a different resonance and effect than the Tibetan
metal singing bowls.
ISBN 90-74597-70-X

YOGA & SOUND
Practical Nada Yoga – Theory and Practice
ISBN 90-74597-91-2

Binkey Kok Publications – Havelte/Holland
www.binkeykok.com
info@binkeykok.com